Harvesting Clouds

Tram Stop Poets
Harvesting Clouds

Harvesting Clouds
ISBN 978 1 76109 025 7
Copyright © text Tram Stop Poets 2020
Editors: Amelia Fielden and Ken Filewood
Cover image: Rohan Buettel

First published 2020 by
Ginninderra Press
PO Box 3461 Port Adelaide 5015 Australia
www.ginninderrapress.com.au

Contents

Foreword	7
Viewing Monet	9
House Under Construction	11
The Listening Pavilion	12
Tanka	13
Cycladic Figure	14
nostalgia in a wineglass	15
The Last Time I Saw Paris	17
water lilies	18
Love	19
Things you should know	20
cradling tears	21
Family Tree	22
Tracking Time	23
At Stanage Edge	24
You weren't available	25
The Hairdresser	26
There comes a time when…	27
Too Many Hours	29
Canvassing a Cure	30
Patient	32
Weather Signs	33
A Winter's Outing	34
Why is it that we watch cricket?	35
One Misstep	36
Straight Line Circle	37
Cloud light	38
Trace	39
The Message	40

Puzzle	41
Bella	42
Old Amy	43
Handwritten notes	45
The trap	47
Tanka	48
Able 1959	49
Stamped with the Caption	50
Tableau with no background music	51
blue	52
Reconciliation	53
Burnout	54
Soon	56
Heatwave 2019	57
Carved in granite	59
Transit	61
Breathing	62
The Dolphin	64
Baranguba	65
Desert sunrise	66
pewter lace unravels	67
Look at the birds of the air…	68
Bruce Ridge	69
Roos at the bushfire	70
Biographies	71
Acknowledgements	74

Foreword

While compiling this anthology of Canberra group Tram Stop Poets, it soon became obvious to me that we had a truly multifarious collection, including traditional pieces, free verse and Japanese forms, as well as ekphrastic, experimental and shaped poems. Such variety is clearly a reflection of our group's poetic diversity, which I believe is its greatest strength. Tram Stop Poets is essentially a workshopping fellowship of both well-known and emerging poets with the aim of critiquing each other's works in a friendly, positive, yet rigorous manner. This allows for substantial cross-fertilisation, where a poet's style and thrust informs the whole, often unconsciously. All of us want to achieve the very best results for our passion and enhance the prospects of having our voices heard in that vibrant, contrary poetry universe.

Several Tram Stop Poets were drawn from the former SOM (School of Music) Poets, which was run by local identity Hazel Hall, in her role as café poet at Biginelli's in the ANU School of Art, Canberra. In January 2019, Hazel asked me to start up a new group to replace SOM Poets, which had many members heavily committed to other poetic pursuits, and I agreed. Thus, the new group (at that time unnamed) came into being at a pivotal meeting on Friday, 1 February 2019.

Finding a name for our group took a while. Many contributions were enthusiastically espoused then trashed with disdain or found to be in use elsewhere. However, while often gazing down from the first floor of the Novotel Canberra during our monthly meetings, we finally found our answer. There it was: Canberra's famous and infamous light rail, both loved and controversial, its bright red carriages gleaming in their novelty, starting, stopping, constantly journeying. An obvious connection. After much discussion, Mira Walker's suggestion of Tram Stop Poets was the most popular.

In compiling this anthology, I would particularly like to thank our editors, Amelia Fielden and Ken Filewood, for their great work and professional approach. Juggling such a disparate range of poems into a meaningful sequence was quite an achievement. I am also grateful to Hazel Hall for convincing me to start up this new group with a similar rationale to SOM Poets, but in my own particular style. Her wisdom and advice continue to be invaluable to me. Thanks also to Rohan Buettel for the image on our cover, which so aptly fits the theme. And, of course, my deep gratitude to all our poets for their enthusiasm for this anthology, their friendship and (most of all!) their great poetry.

So, welcome aboard this debut publication by Tram Stop Poets. We offer what we hope you will find to be a rich, challenging and entertaining anthology. All of the poems in this collection were either previously published or have been workshopped with peers. Every poem has earnt its place. All the poets have given us their best in playing with imaginative ideas and pursuing that elusive dream of harvesting clouds.

          Tony Steven Williams (Convenor, Tram Stop Poets)

Viewing Monet

How did it start: his art of tapping brush on canvas to reveal the ordinary as extraordinary? Could it have been that instant when smoke blended with fog over Charing Cross Bridge, or when a ripple crested in troubled waters, or a leaf fluttered in falling light?

Monet's seminal work, *Impression, Sunrise* was condemned in 1874 as 'sketchy', 'embryonic', 'unfinished wallpaper'. But he continued – and he was not alone. Camille Corot, in the forests of Fontainebleau, was recording nuances of sun and sky, light and shadow. Boudin was painting the air in shades of transparency.

Inveraray
painted in a shroud of light
by Turner
the substance of buildings
lost in the loch

A skilled landscape designer, Monet claimed that his greatest masterpiece was his garden, aspects of which he painted more than 250 times.

his paintings
did not show horizons
yet on the pond
sky floats on the water
a cradle for *nymphéas**

After his death in 1926, Monet's work was not valued highly. The bulk of it was bequeathed by his son to a museum many years later.

long ago
my mother had
a speckled hen
who could well have been
painted by Monet

Carmel Summers

---

* *nymphéas* is the French word for water lilies

House Under Construction

(after the painting by Kazimir Malevich)

there is not much warmth
under a red sun, deconstructed
in separate rectangles
the roofline, solid blocks of colour
diagonals brown, black, blue
lightly affixed
to a thin black wall
early intimations of a wobble
this house under construction
in 1916, abstract, geometric
with a supremacy of feeling
a revolutionary influence
closer to the taste of Trotsky
than another leader
abstraction too dangerous
too ambiguous
formalist and decadent
as Malevich found
arrested, in 1930
afterwards painting
only representations
the house suffering
from the very start
the dilapidation
of dry rot
in the foundations

Rohan Buettel

The Listening Pavilion

(Sculpture at New Acton: *Vortex* by David Jensz)

a mini-lime   pale-striped   slow time
fish collapses creamy on the tongue
yolks spill ellipses on the plate
toward the courtyard centre
wood base shoulders metal sculpture
concentric corrugations
soldered sound waves funnel
the touch of talk
as thoughts embed
spirals of the inner ear
this cochlea enfolds our words
of Aaron and his comrade Rose
the rope he noosed to slip
the tab we pay to stay

Mira Walker

Tanka

on the Ming throne
written one thousand times
longevity –
will this hold back time's march
from his silent tomb

Carmel Summers

Cycladic Figure

So elegant this marble figurine
Impassive, empty, smooth receding face
On abstract forms we can project our dream
For ancient purpose never left its trace

To twenty-first century minds appeal
A flat and modern geometric style
In violin form female shapes reveal
Allusive arms and breasts show sculptor's guile

Was she a pagan mother god of life?
An idol used in sacred rites of death?
Her face once painted shows no sign of strife
Though faded now, she makes us catch our breath

Despite all arguments about her role
She may be nothing but a simple doll

Rohan Buettel

nostalgia in a wineglass

behind bow
glass windows
shapes
glitter
ghostlike
through
spinning
burgundy

slowly, slowly
images
crystallise…

on the beach
I find you –
vermilion
tank top
pulled in
at the waist
long pageboy
cut flowing
and whirling
as you laugh

your
Mediterranean
eyes sing
of the sun
ultra-blue
near-violet
teasing me
over a copper
shoulder

wineglass
you shine!

my fingers
enfold
your narrow
waist
as I tilt you
towards me

our
lips
touch
spice
blackcurrant

slowly
passionately
I empty you
into me

Tony Steven Williams

The Last Time I Saw Paris

A bone-chilling winter. The other day, low-hanging icicles closed the Eiffel Tower to tourists. Snow has fallen again overnight. On the long hill, steep steps to the gleaming dome of Saint Chapelle are crusted with ice as we make our ascent from Montmartre metro station.

The Place des Arts is deserted save for a lone painter in an army greatcoat. Shivering, I glance at his canvas, a skeleton tree shrouded under a blur of impressionistic grey clouds.

Around the corner, in a twisting lane, we find a small bistro beaming light onto the cobbles. Inside, an old-fashioned wood stove crackles with heat.

oak table
by the window, curtained
in red velvet,
two glasses of burgundy
reflecting candle flames

Beyond the window, snowflakes swirl from the darkening sky. Neon lights flicker the name *Le Lapin Qui Rit** above the entrance to a hole-in-the-wall bar across the way.

the rabbit laughs
as my lover lies to me…
Paris,
City of Light, what passions
have smouldered, then died here

Amelia Fielden

* The Laughing Rabbit

water lilies

```
     you                 give              me
   two white          porcelain          stars
 innocent palms    where  chopsticks     r e s t
 little petals cup  the s u n that fills our   morning
 fine-brushed      b l u e  edges  w i t h i n   without
 are waterlines    of  time  spent  together    a p a r t
  a meteor wish   a  c h i n a  g r a s p...  you send me
         water lily outlines on Kuala Lumpur  air letters
                     like the shadows
                       they cast
                           *
```

notes clop
between striped frogs
schoolroom rustle

                                                    a night swan
                                            unfurling to the wingtips
                                                  moon feathers

silver plating –
a wood duck plumps rings
  over water

                                                          Mira Walker

Love

warmth like water
untangles my roots
bulb to daffodil

milkshakes blushed
kissed
in the innocence of spring

no words or touch
only the whisper
of your breath…

your warmth melting yesterday's ice

Sue Donnelly

Things you should know

Deep in the minerals that form your bones
words you've inhaled and ingested,
churned in the enzymatic reaches of your gut,
assimilated and absorbed into platelets,
squeezed through the narrow ventricles of your heart,
that forge your breath, your being.

And now this letter from a stranger who calls you 'mother' –
you turn the letter over, time and time again,
frown as your finger traces a foreign stamp,
troubled by the fleeting sensation of a contracting womb
and a pang in your empty breasts.

There are things you know you should know.

Carmel Summers

cradling tears

gum trees hover
cosseting
a weeping woman

leaves droop
cradling tears
for her baby's form

eucalyptus bleeds
trauma scars
her ravaged body

Sue Donnelly

Family Tree

Family is the tree that finds itself
in documents and photos, it dreams
of the families of the past; the cats
and dogs, the places lived in, walking
beside the sea, the cars driven to loved
ones, the children's first taken steps,
food cooked with love and tears shed
for those lost, arguments too; and
a convict, his shadow known, is
the seed of this story of family.

Janette Pieloor

Tracking Time

We took a shortcut walking kids to school
wearing another way across the park.
The boys, when older, wanting to be cool,
rode their bikes and, eager with the spark
of noisy youth, dug holes, built mounds, and threw
their bikes across those hazards until dark.
They made the course much tougher as they grew
then found more thrills in parking than the park.
Now weeds untrammelled, wild, are free to spread
and years move on; the path becomes unclear
leaving vague signs, uneven to my tread.
I know, in time, the marks will disappear.
Each day, walking the dog, I slowly take
the track less travelled…for old time's sake.

Janne D. Graham

At Stanage Edge

At Stanage Edge, on a blue-rimmed day –
uncertain at the sudden rift
between some, that falls between us all.
Sour-sweet scent of early heather
on the sparse earth between rocks
that I grasp to steady my steps,
cursing an unreliable body.
Granite unrelenting immovable
and the air is shifting.
'It's getting cold,' you say, 'time to go.'
Shadows paint the valley mauve,
nuanced, introspective,
at Stanage Edge, on a blue-rimmed day.
If only we could undo what can't be undone
to rewind that moment.
But time won't turn back
at Stanage Edge, on a blue-rimmed day.

Carmel Summers

You weren't available

I rang to tell you it was my son's birthday today,
tell you I'd rung him early, a toll for that far day
and how he was the first to be fitted into a father's
arms; how he was my alien. He reminds me I say
this each year, at the exact time: he always laughs
then, indulging me, but you weren't available.

I rang to tell you I'd treated myself to a sugar hit
coffee in a dim lit restaurant: I'd walked in as if
a heroine in a mystery novel, then sideways read
my book there as if it held secrets; that the couple
next to me popped champagne, asked me if I'd like
a glass. Of course I said yes, but wiped the rim first.

I rang to tell you I bought myself a chocolate bar,
that it melted on the way home, next to the chunky
meat pie from our favourite bakery; that when I got
back, handsome José came to aerosol those paper
wasps from the deck and throw their nest away,
that it made me sad, but you weren't available.

Janette Pieloor

The Hairdresser

When she said 'Lift our head'
I knew I'd been boxed
in the grey area.
Yes, I wear flat black shoes,
talk to myself and strangers,
smile at babies,
but today I am sixteen again, wearing
a floral dress, walking in high heels
to meet him, for the first time,
my hair flying high.

Janette Pieloor

There comes a time when…

…you are no longer the centre of the family
children are beyond band-aids and rescue
partners and offspring dilute your role
more birthday presents to buy but
Christmas dinner is no longer
your responsibility

…your family cannot believe that you once
water skied on the Canning River
played golf on a billy-goat course in Sydney
skied the slopes of Perisher, at work
survived a knife attack and
many other assaults

…you are the only one interested that you
invited Santa Claus into your Indian hotel room
in Kenya saw a black mamba strike at your door
slept above a hippopotamus orgy on the Zambezi
left your bag, labelled Adventure before Dementia,
at Schiphol Arrivals Hall

…you realise yourself now that
your awards and certificates are no more
than yellowing paper in a drawer
tarnished medals in a box
titles and positions a Google footnote
not one speech on You-tube

…your world begins to narrow
a new building appears and you can't
remember what was there before
friends are recalled through photos, lovers
with a quiet smile, generations of names
begin to blend

…your family has become your centre

Janne D. Graham

Too Many Hours

single again
in a double room
so much space
in which to miss you –
piling pillows on my bed

apricot dawn
spreading across the sky
the sun rises
from beyond the silver sea
where have all the stars gone

if I can live
today without you, then
I can manage
tomorrow, maybe…
doves are cooing somewhere

daily plunge
into an ocean pool
letting the waves
overwhelm my sadness –
on the rocks, tiny crabs

too many hours
until the dark night's dreaming
too many hours
I am alive and you are not
…except in my spirit

Amelia Fielden

Canvassing a Cure

hospital gown
my equilibrium
in a bag

An acrylic artist has been commissioned to paint works for the city hospital. Each image has a different voice like lines of music rising and falling. See these fine white shafts falling from a blue canvas sky, squeezed from the artist's tube like breath from my lungs?

forecast rain
a steady trickle
through my wrist

In the corridor, black electric leads dash across a cobalt sky as huge ivory shapes strut over an icy foreground.

storm trooper
the X-ray machine
comes trundling in

Reception's zig-zag images jump across my mindscape on the back of a paintbrush. In a more gentle approach, patterns outside Theatre are reminiscent of wave-washed sand dunes. Arranged over them are huge red stones worn smooth by the pulse of waves.

recovery room
two pacemakers have
a heart to heart

Now I'm gulping at two strange, psychedelic shapes looming over me. 'Deep breaths,' says a nurse encouragingly.

morphine moon
the many candles
I must blow out

I must be getting better. Hanging near the lift is the wistfulness of an outback landscape in ochre hues. The lines are still present but now they've changed to roads.

flooding my room
with vitamin D
pop-up sun

Can't believe I'm hearing the happy jingle of your keys. On the way to the lift I pay tribute to the artist's inspiration. You murmur soothingly. Say I'm still hallucinating.

hard wired
a week signed off
on the bottom line

Hazel Hall

Patient

hospital nights
bright lights, hard narrow bed
staff chattering –
desperation sleep
finally closes me down

even before
the pale light of dawn
they come
with medications
and blood pressure machines

at my age
fancy wanting my mother,
but who else
could make it all better –
breakfast trolley approaching

in a nightgown
of fiery blue, I question
nurses
as young as my grandchildren
what do *they* know

tree patterns
against an uncertain sky
clouds clustering –
how much longer must I
worry and wonder

Amelia Fielden

Weather Signs

I take you there falsely cheerful
inconsequent chatter about
golden poplars and reddened maples:
colours
of autumn.

I leave you apprehensive
to the care of stethoscopes
and surgery, while long wet weeks
drown me
in time.

I watch you inert, bed-stretched
leasing your life to pumps and plastic
as slivers of sun insinuate:
days dredged
from night.

You are released, the landscape
of your self, scalpel-scarred,
excoriated, weather signs
marking
your time.

You come home through damp
brown, fallen leaves, unseeing,
uncomprehending, as squalls
sweep in
our winter.

Janne D. Graham

A Winter's Outing

they left the doors
of the car open
it was cold
not even in double digits yet
no thought for me
waiting inside
you'd brought me flowers
but even they
were struggling to smile
we were all dressed up
you had on that waistcoat
I bought you years back
but you and your mate
were still standing there
drinking tinnies
full of thoughts
I don't mean to
nag or interrupt
really I don't
but I'm done waiting
today is my funeral

Sue Donnelly

Why is it that we watch cricket?

Obsessively we watch each ball
With tension now the team's behind
The wickets slowly, slowly fall

The pick strikes hard against the wall
The runs are leaden, grimly mined
Obsessively we watch each ball

The batsmen edging at a crawl
Fast bowlers snare them in a bind
The wickets slowly, slowly fall

Threatening time, the umpire's call
Anxiety mounts, crowds the mind
Obsessively we watch each ball

The spinners catch us in their thrall
The runs come dear, but still they grind
The wickets slowly, slowly fall

For fatal fate will seam its pall
Exquisite agony defined
Obsessively we watch each ball
The wickets quick, too quickly fall

Rohan Buettel

One Misstep

stranded
between night and day
in the heat
of a summer bedroom
she pictures waterfalls

waterfalls
all around the rock walls
in the valley
a nervous hiker
stranded on the steep edge

the steep edge
of her frail eighties –
one misstep
and she'll be stranded
in a nursing home

a nursing home
corridor of wheelchairs
entangled
with dreams and nightmares
stranded…

Amelia Fielden

Straight Line Circle

yesterday
talk about going home
cutting nails   shading brows
comfort in the
glint of your eye
your smile as we kiss

today
you almost slip away
lying frail   dreaming
few words last apologies
before fear strands you
in denial and retreat

tomorrow
the motherless child
will be me   struggling
with some simple act of living
will I too call for my mother
near the end as at the beginning?

Mignon Patterson

Cloud light

the almond tree branches blacken
with June rain   eyelets peek
from lichen embroidery in petal swirls

returning Granny's lace to me
roses sketched with cream thread on a web
where lines waver softly with spun fibre

cloud light silvers droplets   beading twigs
its colour is your hair   the white rose
still twirling blooms at her fingertips

you bend to press a stolen flower to my small face
scent billowing from winter wrists   I kiss
your cheek   skin floats a moment between my lips

a plump hug yields to me
through widow's black angora
many winds   mah-jong currents   past him now

was Alexander worth it   iron-framed
to your pale clouds?   today I watch
them blaze as roses and lichen enlace

Mira Walker

Trace

Trace

blind shadows
dream winnowed

slip filtered tiers to
garbled haunts of false witness

thresholds dissolve in shoulds did
till versions distil distant visions

to arrive at a
future already known*

Mignon Patterson

* italics: quotation from *Border Districts*, Gerald Murnane, Giramondo Publishing Company, 2017

The Message

Home again, red light flashing on the machine
Press the button and a woman's voice
Neutral, electronic, strangely slurred

We need to change

                                  Why this need for endless change?

your connection

                                  I would prune a few connections

within 24 to 48 hours

                                  not urgently, just every day

as your IP address has been compromised

                                  too many compromises

from several countries

                                    when one is enough

So we need to change

                                  I would keep things as they are

your IP address and router

                                    although meaningless

which will be free of charge

                                  we always pay in some way

So please press 1

                                                I press 1

to be connected

                                    nothing connects

to the technician

                                no signal, function complete

Rohan Buettel

Puzzle

You are a brain snap, an exercise
of trouble and confusion, you stay
too long and that is not helpful.

You bother the sun and earth with words;
leave them in the air, annoy, ask
where do they all go?

You get me out of bed, remember
something I don't; confuse my dream,
maybe yours.

You play with the leaves, trees
and wind repeatedly; it will get
you into trouble.

Beware the brain.

Janette Pieloor

Bella

knotted
shadows of memory
haunt her body

no longer lithe arabesque
she searches for
toes wrapped in pink satin
bloodied by points

knobbly toes
shuffle in slippers
unrecognisable
except for her name
embroidered in lace

Sue Donnelly

Old Amy

The golden feathers flew
fluttered and faltered:
a canary landed
awkwardly in the dying bush
brown against the grey prison wall.

Old Amy saw it.
Her body tightened and quivered,
a snake with prey in sight.
Her eyes darted:
she alone had seen it.

She slithered towards the wall,
readied, steadied her gaze,
lunged, securing the bird
holding its squirming warmness
secreting it away.

'What's that you've got?' an officer demanded
'Nothing ma'am.'
Feeling nothing; doing nothing;
always nothing.
'Bring it here.' And Amy did.

She opened her scrawny hands to reveal
the grasping beak and pounding heart.
'You can't keep it,' the officer said
looking directly into Amy's eyes
telling her a fact, not giving an order.

Amy turned away. 'It will die,'
the officer called, 'if you do not let it free.'
Old Amy said, 'I know.'
And took the golden bird
to her grey prison cell.

Janne D. Graham

Handwritten notes

we heard the news
unasked and late

his bedroom door
white-faced and hollow-voiced
waits for a question
its chromium lever
rattles and balks

seven torn-out feint-ruled pages
a few times folded, now unfolded
scratched with dark blue ballpoint:
what he had seen
regretted, pleaded, knew

littering the tight, dun pile
twelve strips of silvered plastic
blisters crushed and seedless
rattle when gathered

wet with his ejecta
sheet and blanket stinking
wind him close in arms
as kind as they can be

eyes closed, half-foetal, halfway
turned to face the wall
he seems uncertain now

a cloud of rough-cut verses
covers his recession
hovers while a thoughtful minute passes
over empty cups

Ken Filewood

The trap

at Parliament House, Australia's locked stance:
the thwacking flag hoisted on steel struts

on Manus Island, Australia's closed Centre:
scattered belongings

cheap dormitories   hard floors
press up through thin mattresses

years of hours   in the trap
you lie half bent half stretched

on long lasting nylon in a fierce blue
limbs worn   by all privations

bent arms flung
above your turned face

what does it say?

Mira Walker

Tanka

at the casino
they're waiting for us
mouths open
those colour-lit lions
so loud, so hungry

Tony Steven Williams

Able 1959

Air and Space Museum, Washington, 2016

American-born. Available. Able
fulfilled all requirements to serve.
Did better than creatures before her,
didn't succumb
to Geiger count,
heat, explosion or stress.
Performed the task impeccably,
safely confined in her capsule,
then, on returning,
drew her last breath.

Now an exhibit, bolted and wired
in polyurethane case;
camera above that recorded
each flinch
of straitjacketed tendon and nerve.
She squats as if begging,
spectators extending her use-by date.
A posthumous merit award
for this primate who travelled
three hundred miles into space.

Hazel Hall

Stamped with the Caption

My home is under a railway bridge;
I shuffle about in the dust.
Now and then visitors offer bananas
in hesitant finger-filled fear.
Occasionally they might pay for a ride
then all the iPhones will click.
Souvenirs are available, made from fake leather
or plastic, transported from factories in Dacca.

Each evening I hobble along with my keeper
down to the river to wash,
disco lights on tourist boats winking.
People on deck point and wave.
Activists want me returned to the wild
(plantations have taken its place).
Supporters assembling with slogans on placards
are handcuffed and hurled into cells for their trouble.

Deep in my memory an image persists
where there's nothing but foliage and trees.
Shadows of animals pass in the distance.
I trumpet, but none of them hears.
Wrap me in all the green places you've seen
as years of my life lumber on.
Go home in that tee shirt. The one with my picture,
stamped with the caption I LOVE…

Hazel Hall

Tableau with no background music

Old, odourless ashes co-mingle
with the dusty floor. A gecko hurries
across mud walls, starshine
falls from a hole in the thatch.
The woman, distended belly,
and the sad, bony man wrap
rags around their silent children
(girl and boy). Tomorrow, it is said,
there will be a food drop; tomorrow,
it is said, there will be singing.

Tony Steven Williams

blue

blue as the sprawl of Chamba hills
blue as saffron stars in bloom
belly-blue of an ocean wave
sapphire sky at the cusp of spring
raga-blue of Bhairavi mode
blue as holy Krishna's cloak
blue as an Indian robin's wings
Pangong Lake on a bracing day
blue as the dogs in a Mumbai noon
dyed with toxins from factory swill

Hazel Hall

Reconciliation

I am eager for knowledge
sharing affirmation
sliding into your presence
to take what I can for my future

You speak softly of genocide
gently probe my blood
my ability to understand
and honour hidden history

You draw me in slowly
wait until I am ready
to hear and grasp
we can't change the past

But can embrace here
in our love of red grasses
redemptive remnants amongst
violent alien green

Mignon Patterson

Burnout

elemental
to a tale of tears
iron and lead

preface
to a tale of tanks
one gunshot

eclipsed
by another disaster
breaking news

war stories
filled to the brim
with suffering

my button
is bigger than yours
third world war

how quickly
the world burns out
black rain

long ago
before the rockets
human beings

back at the start
only two are left
to tell the tale

heavy metals
the periodic table
of tears

Hazel Hall

Inspired by 'Brown coloured fairy tale' (chairo-no-otogi-banashi, 茶色のおとぎばなし) by Yamasaki Kayoko. From the translation workshop by Rina Kikuchi, Poetry on the Move, University of Canberra, 2017.

Soon

Deep in a Namibian cavern, huge eggs sit in a cluster as they have for eons. The roar of a lion echoes briefly. Through the jagged mouth of the cave, a waxing gibbous moon faintly illuminates one of the thick black shells.

Many eggs stir, as they do more often now that the years grow warmer, vibrating softly before returning to rest. As each foetus briefly wakes, its brain charges up a little more, sparked by instinctive visions of flight, fire, hunting and gorging. Their growing bodies push ever harder.

it's heating up
hush, tread quietly
don't wake the dragons

Tony Steven Williams

Heatwave 2019

I lie back in the dentist's chair watching waterfalls flowing from the ceiling. In my courtyard, the rhododendron sprouts one rogue mauve blossom from its base. In the extreme heat, the plastic geraniums in the hanging basket are dropping their flowers.

Overheard at the shops: 'How's your new watch?' 'Yeah good, and it saves me taking m'phone out of m'pocket to check the time.'

The annual debate about Australia Day heats up: we forget that 26 January 1808 marks Australia's military coup, the Rum Rebellion – such a fitting anniversary.

A teenager has cut her hair, denied her parents' faith, and advertises on social media that she wants to run away, because her parents will kill her. Western countries vie to offer her asylum.

A soccer player with hard to achieve refugee status in Australia is held overseas on his honeymoon because the country he fled from in terror demands he return. The Australian government is silent.

Our country holds refugees in offshore detention, keeps their inhumane conditions secret then argues it is an effective deterrent to others.

The President of the United States of America wants to build a wall.

The plastic flowers are still dropping.

Mary Oliver
has died: we hope with her
the world keeps in balance

Janne D. Graham

Carved in granite

1

when they tore it down
the Bridge at Waterloo of 1810
gave up a pair of grease-dull stones
now lodged as foreign bodies
in a span we call 'The Commonwealth'

neat amid grey masonry,
where motor-dust has kept
the tracks of gushing fluids
they overlook the smell
abandoned bottles, unswept leaves
a brown and shallow lake

2

beside the bike path, pencil poplars
where the wind slaps scum to froth
against a concrete shore
another block juts ankle-high
from close-cropped weeds

its carven cross, as long as my hand
off-centre, listing on one black and polished face
all they could do for their tragic dead
the plaque explains at length and ends
'Her name will live forever
in these stones'

3

home is deck-boards flexing
keys ajingle, screen door squealing, shaking loose
the cabin sounding like a drum

alive to numbers, I have carried
date and age of death this far
but not her name, eternal, carved in stone

I wonder how the ones who lived there
under blue-green gums now drowned
had marked their stones

Ken Filewood

Transit

                        quanta
                        gauge

            star   sun

      moon   earth

tide   wave

    river   cloud

          heart   breath

                       drip drop
                       tick tock

Mignon Patterson

Breathing

This weekend morning from a rocky headland
grey-dayed north of Sydney
at the wavery spot where a rainbow nudges water
a sudden spout –
a great southern whale breathes out.
Grounded, on algae-speckled clumps of granite
I breathe in.

In this world where rainbows don't quite kiss the land
my lungs absorb molecules that have loitered
in coastal banksia
privet and commuters on the Bankstown line.
Carbon that infuses my brain, will exit as dioxides
to be inhaled, along with failing economies in the tabloid press.

Mist blurs divides of sea and sky
my eyes scan for movement
an instinct, as with breathing
always the discontinuities –
the gasp, the sigh, breathlessness
our navigation through channels of interpretation.

Too easy to ignore that space between breaths
between the out and the in
that bread and butter space
where we hide tears in spoons of Weetbix
shroud insecurity in an off-the-peg suit
dream to be different, but never quite dare.

I watch for shadows midst the waves
for the breach of an arched fin
a scream of air
and for a moment, I belong in a place
where molecules depart, combine, reconfigure
shielding our samenesses
forming our differences
as we breathe.

Carmel Summers

The Dolphin

One morning drive, a lonely ocean way
The blinding sun dazzling from monster swell
I glancing saw grey shape emerge through spray
Down precipitous slope tail thrusts propel
To quickly execute a bottom turn
And power up the face of glassy wave
Then reach the crest and dive over the churn
To disappear into the roiling lave

A dolphin surfs inside a mounting surge
With streamlined shape to minimise the drag
Slide through laminar planes, waters diverge
Seen once, human surfers no longer brag
Superb mastery, a dolphin at play
Being itself, the most perfect display

Rohan Buettel

Baranguba

ancient Nut springs from Gulaga
dances across the glittering island
pivoting on twin granite sentinels,
fin echoes calling all to feast
as bait fish race wind and whales

baby chicks melt into warm rocks
wait for their mothers to win
the howling greedy dogfight overhead,
the little red hawk patiently
patrols melaleucas for gale tossed finches

sky mirrors roiling sea,
we poke the storm wrack
startle dozing seals and
fat crabs in ruby anemones

with sun and moon poised on each horizon
nautilus ride swell swollen weed forests,
the mass lunar glow
quickens in the gelatinous bay

smoke and dust haze the coast

Mignon Patterson

Desert sunrise

the torch of dawn has silenced stars
and stained the sky with greens and browns
of tea-steeped waters lying limp
on tawny sand

low clouds in swales are feathers lit
with fuchsia fires blown soft and bright
from fusing wires

night-air lingers cool and dim
its broad breast pressed upon
the desert's rim

it kisses the skin of arms and legs,
carries the voice of a cockatoo
and clinging breathes

the flinty dust of orange dunes
and spinifex, and oil of mulga
leaves and bark

the purple skirt of night drinks light
grows pale and paler, starts to blue:
for soon the sun will cut the hem
its white gold needle prick my eye

Ken Filewood

pewter lace unravels

what shape of bird
keens everything new
this full moon
half-known impulse
you resolve for flight

west wind peels
wetness from my eyes
finding
only your half image
in wattle bush shade

a storm bird
bamboo flute music
calls
rising and tailing
i am   i am   here

nimbus face
with pewter lace unravelling
open
to the burning iris
winking in the drift

a hump of light
riding each birch leaf
gusts tumble
across the midnight grove –
your strobe of moonbright

Mira Walker

Look at the birds of the air…

vermilion breast
in a camouflage of leaves
King parrot
high on an ash tree –
the world from my window

speckled wattlebirds
framed by crimson-petaled
camellias –
my mother always made me
look pretty for school dances

rose pink grey-cloaked
galahs hang upside down
from the swings
in the childless playground –
nearby, teenagers texting

unconcerned
at my dog's approach,
glossy magpies
striding the dew, tuning up,
bright eyes meet bright eyes

in wild grass
two Eastern rosellas
foraging –
so long since his death
I've been blind to beauty

Amelia Fielden

* New Testament, Matthew 6:26–34

Bruce Ridge

the country is a ghost-ground
spilled from a drowned man's inks:
still, liquid neutrals; crisp lines
smooth and scattered, bent

inhale charcoal, termites, rotting;
panicked ants and oils of trees;
kicked clay, a breath of fractured shale

the gums look out through slitted eyes;
half-shadow beards, hands, heads
and shoulders dislocate and drooping;
filled with a yogi's hard-pent vigour
standing by to let play occult fire

Ken Filewood

Roos at the bushfire

Late afternoon in the forest,
rolling, roaring air,
super-dry, crisping hot.
Treetops bend like hair under a drier
on full blast, full heat.
Incandescent reds and yellows strobe
dark rolling eyes. A branch cracks
with a drummer's thump –
jumping, brown shadows fracture
the shallow water of a stream.

A moment of sanity as the wind drops.
Shock-still, ears outlined in fire,
necks heaving upwards –
they're sniffing acid air for escape,
long forgotten the mindless
bounding flight to this strange
terrible place. Undergrowth,
burn control, park management
and politics have no meaning here.

They know only that the sun has gone.

Tony Steven Williams

Biographies

Rohan Buettel spent his early years in Brisbane and moved to Canberra where he spent three decades contributing to public service. His poetry has been published in *Quadrant*.

Sue Donnelly: storyteller, short story writer, performance poet. Editor on numerous poetry committees. Facilitator of various writing workshops for primary, high school and adults. Performance poet at Federation Square, Box Hill Theatre and various festivals. Regular poet on radio. Poetry and short stories published in 14 anthologies. Poetry book *Heartfelt Moments* published by Ginninderra Press (2014).

Amelia Fielden is a translator, collaborator and editor, who is also a keen writer of Japanese poetic forms in English. She has been published in journals and anthologies worldwide. Eight of her original collections have appeared, the most recent being *These Purple Years* (2018).

Ken Filewood designs games that depict imaginary worlds. His poems celebrate nature and draw attention to human suffering.

Janne D. Graham returned to poetry at 70, first sharing reading in a U3A group and later writing. As a 'left-brain' person she was keen to rediscover her creativity. After winning second prize for 'Old Amy' she has decided to call herself a poet.

Hazel Hall is an award-winning Australian poet and musicologist. Her latest collections are *Step by Step*, a t'ai chi collaboration with Angie Egan (Picaro Press 2019), *Moonlight Over the Siding* (Interactive Press 2019), a collection for dog lovers, *You are Her Words*, with Canadian artist Karen Bailey (2019) and *Severed Web*, a climate change collection with Australian artist Deborah Faeyrglenn (Picaro Press 2020).

Mignon Patterson is enjoying her first loves of poetry, music and physics after a career fashioned from various forms of writing. After living in Canberra for more than 35 years, she spends as much time as possible in remote bush and fresh air.

Janette Pieloor is an established Australian poet with more than 30 years of publications in Australian poetry anthologies, magazines and journals, including in *The Best Australian Poems* 2011 and *Australian Poetry Journal* (2014). She published her first poetry collection *Ripples Under the Skin* in 2015. Her new poetry collection *Then and Now* was published in 2019 by Recent Work Press.

Carmel Summers is a Canberra poet and writer. Her first book of responsive tanka, *The last day before snow*, written with eight Australian poets, was awarded the ACT Publishing Award for Poetry in 2017. Her work appears in a number of collections and journals in Australia and overseas. She has an MA in Creative Writing from Macquarie University.

Mira Walker's poetic gaze shifts from fairy wrens to froglets, ochre dust to ant feelers, and moon phases to the blues of blown glass. She is an Australian poet based in Canberra. Her poetry is published in a range of international and Australian journals and anthologies. Mira particularly enjoys creating visual and shaped poems, haiku and tanka.

Tony Steven Williams is a poet, short-fiction author and song writer with work published in anthologies, newspapers, print and online magazines, and broadcast on the radio. Ginninderra Press published his debut poetry collection *Sun and Moon, Light and Dark* in 2018.

Acknowledgements

'House Under Construction' was published in *Quadrant*, November 2019.
'The Last Time I Saw Paris' in *Haibun Today*, Autumn 2019.
'water lilies' (flower body) in *Pour Me a Poem*, Watson Poets, 2014.
'water lilies' (night swan haiku) in *cattails*, April 2019.
'water lilies' (silver-plated haiku) in *Echidna Tracks* Issue 3: Insects, Animals, Birds and Fish, September 2019.
'You weren't available' in *Australian Poetry Journal 2014*, Volume 4, Issue 2.
'Too Many Hours' in *Ribbons* (Journal of the Tanka Society of America), Autumn/Winter 2019.
'Canvassing a Cure' in Krishnamurthy, Srikaanth (ed.), *Ephemerae* 1, 2017.
'Patient' in *Kokako* 31, September 2019.
'Why is it that we watch cricket?' in *Quadrant,* April 2019.
'One Misstep' in *red lights journal*, USA, June 2019.
'Cloud light' in *Pour Me a Poem*, Watson Poets, 2014.
'The Message' in *Quadrant*, November 2019.
'Old Amy' in *A Feast of Poetry* 2013, Cooma Poetry Competition, 2013 (second prize, open section).
'Able 1959' in *The Canberra Times* (Panorama Section), October 2018.
'Stamped with the Caption' in *Wild*, Joan Fenney (ed.), Ginninderra Press, 2018.
'Burnout' in Krishnamurthy, Srikaanth (ed.), *Ephemerae* 3, 2017.
'Soon' in *KYSO Flash*, Issue 12, August 2019.
'Breathing' shortlisted for the Blake Poetry Prize, 2012.
'The Dolphin' in *Quadrant,* November 2019.
'Look at the birds of the air…' in *International Tanka*, Japan, October 2019.

www.ingramcontent.com/pod-product-compliance
Lightning Source LLC
Chambersburg PA
CBHW062152100526
44589CB00014B/1794